EUROPEAN COUNTRIES TODAY
DENMARK

EUROPEAN COUNTRIES TODAY

TITLES IN THE SERIES

Austria	Italy
Belgium	Netherlands
Czech Republic	Poland
Denmark	Portugal
France	Spain
Germany	Sweden
Greece	United Kingdom
Ireland	European Union Facts & Figures

EUROPEAN COUNTRIES TODAY
DENMARK

Dominic J. Ainsley

MASON CREST

Mason Crest
450 Parkway Drive, Suite D
Broomall, Pennsylvania PA 19008
(866) MCP-BOOK (toll free)

Copyright © 2019 by Mason Crest, an imprint of National Highlights, Inc. All rights reserved. No part of this publication may be reproduced or transmitted in any form or by any means, electronic or mechanical, including photocopying, recording, taping, or any information storage and retrieval system, without permission in writing from the publisher.

First printing
9 8 7 6 5 4 3 2 1

ISBN: 978-1-4222-3981-0
Series ISBN: 978-1-4222-3977-3
ebook ISBN: 978-1-4222-7796-6

Library of Congress Cataloging-in-Publication Data

Names: Ainsley, Dominic J., author.
Title: Denmark / Dominic J. Ainsley.
Description: Broomall, Pennsylvania : Mason Crest, 2019. | Series: European countries today | Includes index.
Identifiers: LCCN 2018007572 (print) | LCCN 2018016014 (ebook) | ISBN 9781422277966 (eBook) | ISBN 9781422239810 (hardback)
Subjects: LCSH: Denmark--Juvenile literature.
Classification: LCC DL109 (ebook) | LCC DL109 .A36 2019 (print) | DDC 948.9--dc23
LC record available at https://lccn.loc.gov/2018007572

Printed in the United States of America

Cover images
Main: *Copenhagen.*
Left: *Smørrebrød (Danish open sandwich).*
Center: *Statue of the Little Mermaid.*
Right: *Danish folk dancers.*

QR CODES AND LINKS TO THIRD-PARTY CONTENT

You may gain access to certain third-party content ("Third- Party Sites") by scanning and using the QR Codes that appear in this publication (the "QR Codes"). We do not operate or control in any respect any information, products, or services on such Third-Party Sites linked to by us via the QR Codes included in this publication, and we assume no responsibility for any materials you may access using the QR Codes. Your use of the QR Codes may be subject to terms, limitations, or restrictions set forth in the applicable terms of use or otherwise established by the owners of the Third-Party Sites. Our linking to such Third-Party Sites via the QR Codes does not imply an endorsement or sponsorship of such Third-Party Sites or the information, products, or services offered on or through the Third-Party Sites, nor does it imply an endorsement or sponsorship of this publication by the owners of such Third-Party Sites.

CONTENTS

Denmark at a Glance	6
Chapter 1: Denmark's Geography & Landscape	11
Chapter 2: The Government & History of Denmark	23
Chapter 3: The Danish Economy	43
Chapter 4: Citizens of Denmark: People, Customs & Culture	55
Chapter 5: The Famous Cities of Denmark	71
Chapter 6: A Bright Future for Denmark	81
Chronology	90
Further Reading & Internet Resources	91
Index	92
Picture Credits & Author	96

KEY ICONS TO LOOK FOR:

Words to Understand: These words with their easy-to-understand definitions will increase the reader's understanding of the text while building vocabulary skills.

Sidebars: This boxed material within the main text allows readers to build knowledge, gain insights, explore possibilities, and broaden their perspectives by weaving together additional information to provide realistic and holistic perspectives.

Educational Videos: Readers can view videos by scanning our QR codes, providing them with additional content to supplement the text. Examples include news coverage, moments in history, speeches, iconic sports moments, and much more!

Text-Dependent Questions: These questions send the reader back to the text for more careful attention to the evidence presented there.

Research Projects: Readers are pointed toward areas of further inquiry connected to each chapter. Suggestions are provided for projects that encourage deeper research and analysis.

DENMARK AT A GLANCE

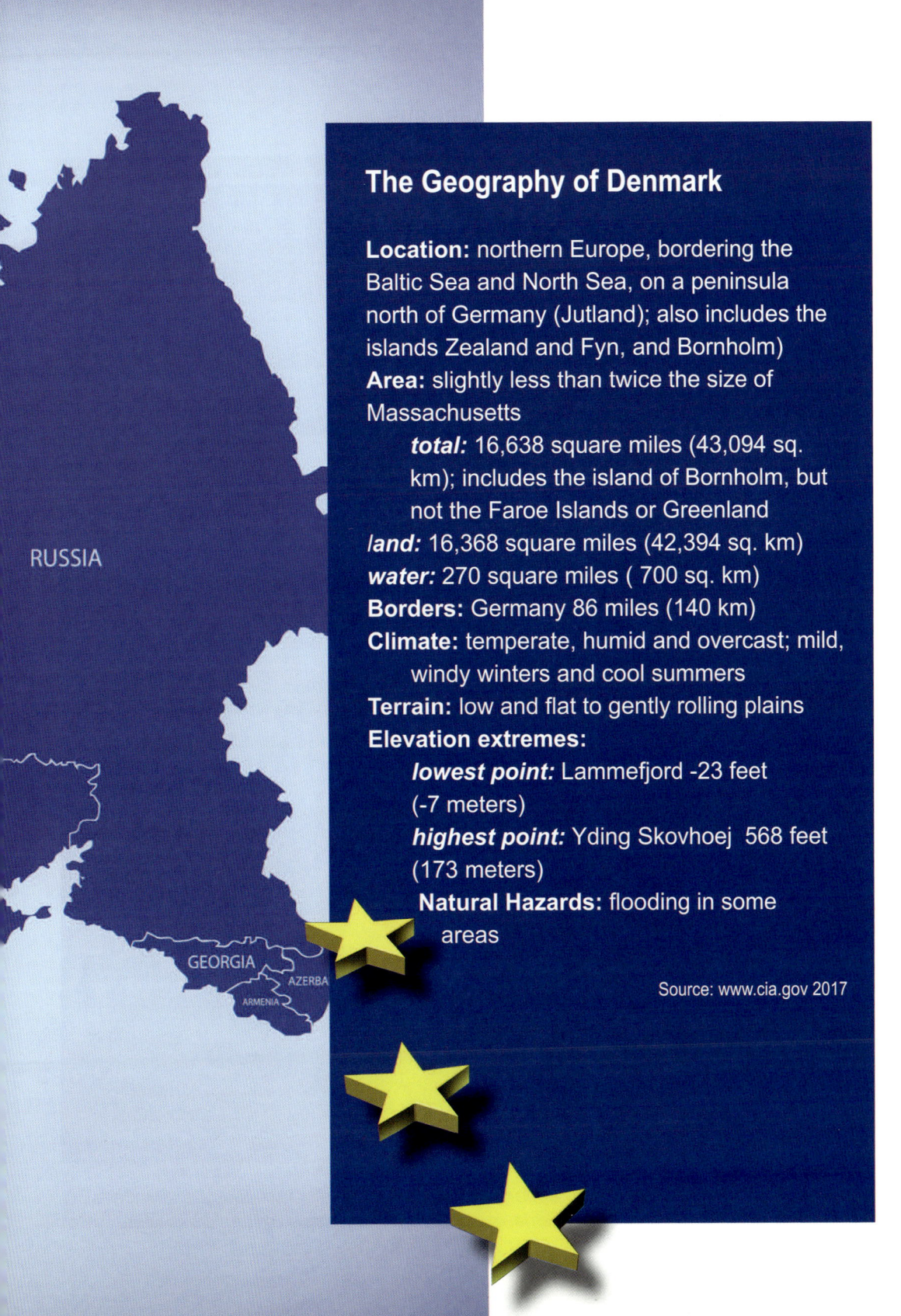

The Geography of Denmark

Location: northern Europe, bordering the Baltic Sea and North Sea, on a peninsula north of Germany (Jutland); also includes the islands Zealand and Fyn, and Bornholm)

Area: slightly less than twice the size of Massachusetts

total: 16,638 square miles (43,094 sq. km); includes the island of Bornholm, but not the Faroe Islands or Greenland

land: 16,368 square miles (42,394 sq. km)

water: 270 square miles (700 sq. km)

Borders: Germany 86 miles (140 km)

Climate: temperate, humid and overcast; mild, windy winters and cool summers

Terrain: low and flat to gently rolling plains

Elevation extremes:

lowest point: Lammefjord -23 feet (-7 meters)

highest point: Yding Skovhoej 568 feet (173 meters)

Natural Hazards: flooding in some areas

Source: www.cia.gov 2017

DENMARK AT A GLANCE

Flag of Denmark

The mainland part of Denmark is an extension of the North German Plain, known as the Jutland Peninsula. Denmark also includes 406 islands, of which 89 are inhabited. Denmark is one of the oldest monarchies in Europe and at one time had a large empire. The Faroe Islands and Greenland are still dependencies, but have a large degree of autonomy. The Danish flag is possibly one of the oldest flags in continuous use. It dates back to 1219, when King Waldemar II saw a vision of a white cross in the sky before the Battle of Lyndanisse, the red background representing the sullen evening sky of that night. The flag is known as the *Dannebrog* (the spirit of Denmark), the off-center cross being common to all the flags of the Scandinavian countries.

ABOVE: *The Nyhavn waterfront in Copenhagen is famous for its outdoor cafés. Once a busy commercial port, it is now pedestrianized and a perfect place for tourists to dine.*

EUROPEAN COUNTRIES TODAY: DENMARK

The People of Denmark

Population: 5,593,785
Ethnic groups: Scandinavian, Inuit, Faroese, German, Turkish, Iraqi, Polish, Syrian
Age structure:
    0–14 years 16.58%
    15–64 years 64.46%
    65 years and above 18.96%
Population grown rate: 0.22%
Birth rate: 10.4 births/1,000 pop.
Death rate: 10.3 deaths/1,000 pop.
Migration rate: 2.1 migrants/1,000 pop.
Infant mortality rate: 4 deaths/1,000 live births
Life expectancy at birth:
    Total population: 79.4 years
    Male: 77 years
    Female: 82 years
Total fertility rate: 1.73 children born/woman
Religions: Evangelical Lutheran 76%, other Protestant and Roman Catholic 20%, Muslim 4%
Languages: Danish, Faroese, Greenlandic, German
Literacy rate: 99%

Source: www.cia.gov 2017

Words to Understand

glaciers: Large bodies of ice moving slowly down a slope or valley.

ice age: A period of widespread glaciation.

migratory: Moving from one place to another.

BELOW: Bornholm is a beautiful island located in the Baltic Sea south of Sweden and north of Poland. The island is a popular tourist destination.

Chapter One
DENMARK'S GEOGRAPHY & LANDSCAPE

Hallo Goddag! Welcome to Denmark. An ancient land, now admired for its cornfields, bridges, and interesting cities, Denmark is a small but prominent member of the European Union (EU). About three times the size of Long Island, with a population about two-thirds as large as that of New York City, Denmark is a nation of nearly 5.6 million people. It is located in Western Europe, north of Germany and west of Sweden.

Historically, the Danes have been a seafaring people, owing perhaps to the nation's location between the North and Baltic seas. Today, Denmark is comprised of the mainland of the Jutland Peninsula, as well as a network of more then four hundred islands, most of which are connected to the mainland by bridges or ferries. The capital of Copenhagen lies on the largest of the islands, Zealand.

Plains, Hills, and Moraines

The landscape seen in Denmark today is largely a product of glacial activity that occurred during the last **ice age**. As the ice advanced and retreated over the centuries, hills of salt, sand, and gravel were pushed up, and other areas were flattened. Runoff

ABOVE: *Fishing trawlers in the fishing port of Havneby on the island of Rømø.*

DENMARK'S GEOGRAPHY & LANDSCAPE

Educational Video

This 10-minute video provides a brief insight into Denmark's geography. Scan the QR code with your phone to watch!

ABOVE: *Hirtshals is a coastal town and seaport on the island of Vendsyssel-Thy at the top of the Jutland Peninsula. It is located on the Skagerrak Strait.*

EUROPEAN COUNTRIES TODAY: DENMARK

ABOVE: *Sand dunes at Blaavand on the North Sea coast of Jutland.*

from melting ice caused shallow depressions and valleys. As a result, the landscape in Denmark is largely flat with gently rolling hills.

Although Jutland has some bedrock, and some can also be found on the island of Bornholm, the vast majority of the country is made up of moraine. (Moraines are a sandy mixture of clay, soil, and stones left behind by glaciers.) There is also an abundance of salt and chalk in some areas of Denmark, which are among the country's few natural resources. Due to its location between the North and Baltic seas, Denmark also boasts many beautiful beaches and rich coastal habitats. These areas are home to a wide variety of aquatic life and provide many valuable harvests for the nation's fishermen.

Visitors to Denmark often comment that the country looks like a well-tended garden. That is because after so many centuries of human habitation and

DENMARK'S GEOGRAPHY & LANDSCAPE

Burnet Rose

The burnet rose grows in abundance in the sandunes and limestone areas along the Danish coastline. It is a very old rose, that has been present in Denmark for thousands of years. Usually growing to about 39 inches (100 cm) tall, it has cream-white or pale pink flowers that have a wonderful fragrance. It manages to survive in the sandy soils of the region—probably because its long roots can reach nutrients deep down in the soil. The small berries (or hips) it produces have long been used for making preserves and wine. The burnet rose blossoms in June and July.

agriculture, little natural forest land remains in Denmark. Instead, the Danes enjoy what is commonly known as a cultural landscape, where the landscape has been permanently altered by human activities. As much as 65 percent of Denmark's land is used for agriculture. The result is that a drive across the countryside reveals neatly divided fields of grain, punctuated by small towns, and occasionally a small green forest or a meadow covered in wildflowers.

Rivers and Lakes

Denmark claims many interconnecting rivers, canals, and lakes. The most important river is the river Guden, both a tourist attraction and a busy transport waterway that flows across Jutland. The Odense, the Stor, the Varde, and the Skjern are other important rivers.

EUROPEAN COUNTRIES TODAY: DENMARK

ABOVE: The Køge River is small river that drains into the Bay of Køge on the east coast of Zealand. Tourists can take the Køge River Path, which is picturesque and interesting.

DENMARK'S GEOGRAPHY & LANDSCAPE

ABOVE: The city of Silkeborg in Eastern Jutland is divided north and south by the lake of Silkeborg Langsø, which at the eastern side of the city discharges into the river Guden.

   The Danish landscape is also dotted with freshwater lakes. The **glaciers** that shaped this land in the ice ages left behind many of these small lakes. Others are manmade, formed by the many dams and canals Danes have created to make their very moist soil suitable for agriculture.
   Denmark has a cool, temperate climate with plentiful rainfall. Because of its proximity to the sea, the entire nation enjoys especially mild weather. The temperature rarely dips below 30°F (-1°C) in the winter and averages about 57°F (16.5°C) during the summer.

EUROPEAN COUNTRIES TODAY: DENMARK

Danish weather is also highly variable; over a period of a few days, the weather may change from steady rain that precedes a warm front, to sunnier, misty weather, possibly with a little drizzle as the warmer air moves in. During the summer, sudden, brief thunderstorms are common, especially in the afternoons. Overall, Denmark has about 180 days of precipitation each year, meaning that Danes expect rain or snow for about half of the year.

ABOVE: *Roskilde Fjord features one of Denmark's most beautiful and diverse landscapes. The narrow inlet, which extends 25 miles (40 km) into the Zealand landscape, is dotted with many small islands and islets, and is home to a rich and undisturbed flora and fauna.*

DENMARK'S GEOGRAPHY & LANDSCAPE

Cormorant

The cormorant is a common species found in Denmark along seashores and in lakes and reservoirs, where its skill at catching fish often causes it to come into conflict with anglers. A generally, long-necked, almost snake-like bluish-black bird, but with attractive subtle marbling on its wings and a large yellow bill, the cormorant also has white cheeks and thigh patches when breeding. It swims well, rarely venturing far from land, and dives from the surface to hunt for fish, bringing big prey to the surface before swallowing it. After a fishing expedition the cormorant will often find a suitable wooden post, rock, or similar elevated site on which to perch. Cormorants breed in colonies, with nests often built on trees or cliffs.

Trees, Plants, and Wildlife

In the past, much of Denmark was covered with rich beech and oak forests. Over the centuries these forests have largely disappeared as agriculture has grown. As farmers have cleared more and more land for cultivation, the landscape has been permanently altered, and less than 10 percent of these original forests remain in Denmark.

Even with the elimination of most of its forests, Denmark is still home to a wide variety of flora. Currently the country has more than 1,500 species of plants. Most common are the many varieties of wildflowers, berries, and grasses. Danish wildlife has also been affected by the dwindling woodlands,

EUROPEAN COUNTRIES TODAY: DENMARK

ABOVE: Demark consists of many islands and therefore has long stretches of coastline. Its dunes support many hardy species of plants that have adapted to a wet climate and poor soil.

DENMARK'S GEOGRAPHY & LANDSCAPE

ABOVE: *In Denmark, much of the coastal marshland has been drained for agriculture.*

EUROPEAN COUNTRIES TODAY: DENMARK

and most of the species currently listed as endangered require a forest habitat. The draining of marshland for agriculture has also caused the elimination of some unique habitats and is the reason that more than one-third of the nation's amphibians are now in danger of extinction. Still, many animals thrive in the Danish countryside: one can find foxes, hares, hedgehogs, and house martins, in addition to an array of other birds. The most common of these are the house sparrow, great tit, and starling.

In the coastal waters, marine life is rich and varied. Jellyfish and copepods float offshore, and porpoise, cod, herring, and plaice swim freely. Cockles, mussels, crabs, and starfish are common, as are seals and a wide assortment of seabirds. Danish waters are of international importance as a resting place for up to 20 percent of all the world's **migratory** sea birds. As is the case all across Denmark, strict environmental laws protect the environment and all plant and animal life that may be endangered by the activities of human beings.

Text-Dependent Questions

1. What are Denmark's most important rivers?

2. What animals are commonly found in Denmark?

3. What percentage of land in Demark is used for agriculture?

Research Project

Find out why Denmark has a temperate climate. Explain what kinds of weather conditions it has in summer and in winter. Name some other countries that have similar climates around the world.

21

Words to Understand

mummified: A preserved dead body, treated with oils and then wrapped in cloth.

pagan: A religion based on the worship of nature or the earth.

Vikings: Members of a group of Scandinavian people who attacked the coasts of Europe in the eighth to tenth centuries.

BELOW: Lindholm Høje (Lindholm Hills) is a major Viking burial site and former settlement situated to the north of, and overlooking, the city of Aalborg.

Chapter Two
THE GOVERNMENT & HISTORY OF DENMARK

Denmark has a rich and ancient history. For the Danes, the continuity of their language, history, and culture is a source of pride and the basis for their strong sense of national identity. In modern times, Denmark stands as a strong, democratic country, a prominent member of the United Nations, and a central figure in the EU. As a nation, Denmark is committed to peace and shares good relations with other countries. The Danish people are equally proud of their history and the way in which their small country has embraced the changes that the twenty-first century has brought.

Denmark in Ancient Times

Five thousand years ago, most of the inhabitants of Danish lands made their home near the coast and lived on fish and shellfish. They supplemented these foods by hunting seals and game, which provided skins for clothing and shelter as well as food. In those times, a dense forest blanketed most of the countryside.

ABOVE: *Charlemagne by Albrecht Dürer.*

23

THE GOVERNMENT & HISTORY OF DENMARK

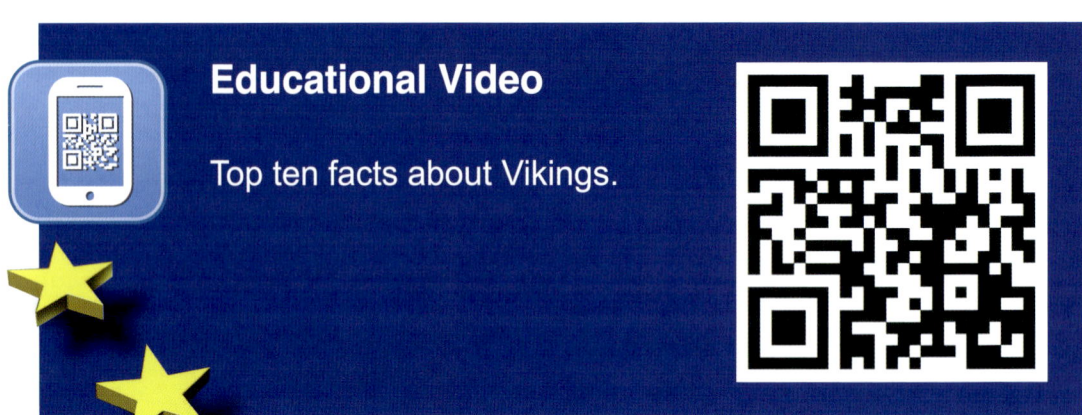

Educational Video

Top ten facts about Vikings.

The earliest people of Denmark worshipped the ancient **pagan** gods, and when an important chief passed away, he was laid to rest in a burial mound, together with his slaves, animals, wives, and other belongings. In modern times, these graves have been found scattered around the country, and by carefully studying their contents, researchers have been able to piece together many details of the daily lives of these ancient people. A few bodies have been found **mummified** in bogs, so we know a great deal about how these people looked, how they dressed, and even what they ate.

Around 500 CE, a tribe calling itself the Danes migrated from Sweden with the intent of conquering what is now Denmark. Their language, preserved in a few ancient writings, was a northern German dialect, which already featured many important differences from German itself. Modern Danish is very different from both Swedish and German in tone and spelling, although enough similarities exist for most Danes to understand Swedish.

In Germany, to the south, the Franks emerged as the most powerful tribe in the region. Charlemagne, a Frank and the greatest ruler of his era, built an empire that extended over Germany, France, and much of central Italy. The Franks began to push north, hoping to further expand their holdings. Around 800, the Danish Viking Godfred took up the challenge posed by the Franks and established the boundaries of his country, now known as Denmark. Over the next three hundred years, Vikings would play a prominent role in many of the most important and dramatic events in European history.

EUROPEAN COUNTRIES TODAY: DENMARK

The Age of the Vikings

The bold **Vikings** ruled the North Sea, the Baltic Sea, and the continental rivers adjacent to them for a long period of time. Known for their sense of adventure and lack of fear, the Vikings were some of Europe's earliest explorers. On one of their trips they even visited North America, hundreds of years before a similar journey would make Christopher Columbus famous. Several Danish towns that began as Viking settlements are now over one thousand years old. Copenhagen, the Danish capital, which started out as a small fishing village with some traders and a marketplace, was founded more than eight hundred years ago.

ABOVE: *A reconstruction of a Viking house at Lejre.*

The Jelling Stones

The Jelling stones (Jellingstenene) are massive carved rune stones from the tenth century situated in the town of Jelling. The smaller of the two Jelling stones was raised by King Gorm the Old in memory of his wife Thyra. The larger of the two stones was raised by King Gorm's son, Harald Bluetooth in memory of his parents. It was also to celebrate his conquest of Denmark and Norway, and the conversion of the Danes to Christianity. The runic inscriptions on these stones are considered to be the best in Denmark.

The stones are on display next to Jelling Church. In 2016 the stones became a UNESCO World Heritage Site. Due to vandalism and cracking, the decision was made to incase them in glass. Pictured left are the stones with and without their glass cases.

THE GOVERNMENT & HISTORY OF DENMARK

Technologically, the Vikings had a great advantage over neighboring peoples; namely, their fast, seaworthy warships. With their open, square-rigged vessels, the Vikings sailed Europe's coastal waters, acting as traders, pirates, and colonizers. Coastal monasteries and abbeys lived in fear of attack from these pagan seafarers who did not hesitate to raid Christian houses of worship for valuable gold and silver. The word *Viking*, which means "one who fights at sea," can be found on several runic stones from that period.

Initially, the Vikings operated as a loosely united set of tribes, with authority in the hands of one chief or another. However, by 900, Denmark was united under the rule of one king. King Gorm the Old established the Danish monarchy, and the country has continued as a monarchy in one form or another ever since.

ABOVE: *King Gorm learns of the death of his son, Canut. Painting by August Carl Vilhelm Thomsen.*

The Monarchy

King Gorm the Old was succeeded by his son King Harald Bluetooth, who ruled from 950 to 985. King Harald's rule is recorded on the famous Jelling Stone. Sometimes referred to as Denmark's birth certificate, the enormous stone features a depiction of Jesus on the cross and has a runic inscription carved on its side. The stone states that King Harald converted the Danes to Christianity. In fact, the Danes did begin to convert to Roman Catholicism around this time. Denmark remained Roman Catholic until the Protestant Reformation occurred in neighboring Germany in the early 1500s. At that time, Denmark became predominantly Lutheran, and it remains so to this day.

EUROPEAN COUNTRIES TODAY: DENMARK

ABOVE: A relief dating to c. 1200 of Harald being baptized by Poppo the Monk.

THE GOVERNMENT & HISTORY OF DENMARK

ABOVE: *King Frederik I of Denmark, anonymous.*

Denmark continued to be ruled by Harald's descendants until the last king of the line died without an heir in 1448. At this time, the monarch was chosen by an election limited to the royal family, though not to males only. In 1448, Count Christian of Oldenborg was elected king of Denmark under the name Christian I. His direct successors from the House of Oldenburg adopted alternately the names of Frederik and Christian, beginning with the election of Frederik I in 1523. The elective monarchy continued until 1660, when Frederik III decreed a hereditary monarchy for Denmark and Norway, which at the time was also under his rule.

Perhaps the most beloved monarch in Danish history was King Christian IV, memorialized today in the Danish national anthem. Although the anthem portrays King Christian as a victorious warrior, in truth he lost as many battles as he won. Fortunately, his greatest legacy is not his military record, but rather his lavish support of the arts and architecture. Throughout King Christian's reign, he contributed enormously to the development of Danish architecture, painting, music, and commerce. Many of Denmark's magnificent Renaissance buildings would not have existed without the financial support of the king.

Danish Nationalism and the Constitution

By 1806, the French general Napoleon Bonaparte had dissolved Germany's Holy Roman Empire completely and was working to expand his own empire

EUROPEAN COUNTRIES TODAY: DENMARK

across Europe. The defeat awakened a sense of nationalism in many European nations, prompting discussions of linguistic and cultural awareness throughout the people of Europe. It also renewed cries for political freedom and democracy that had begun with the revolution in the United States of America, and closer to home with the overthrow of the French monarchy.

These new political ideas had resonance for the Danish people, who were among the most prosperous and best educated in Europe at that time. Political parties began to form, and a movement began in support of giving the Danish people a voice in their government and establishing basic civil liberties for all citizens.

In 1848, Denmark's Liberal Party called on King Frederik VII to renounce the system of absolute monarchy and form a democratically elected national assembly, which would then draft a constitution to establish the rights of all Danish citizens. The resulting constitution was signed into force on June 5, 1849, and was extremely liberal for its time. Overnight, Denmark became the most democratic and freest nation in Europe. Unfortunately, the constitution was difficult to enforce, mostly because the king was not willing to give up his power. In the end, the entire monarchy was restructured, and Danish citizens received many basic rights, which they still possess.

In the years that followed, the new system of government led to widespread changes in Danish society. Peasants and men of great wealth and education were now equal under the law, and soon the common people were holding elected office. Women were granted full suffrage in 1915. Denmark remained neutral throughout World War I, although it

ABOVE: *Christian IV of Denmark by Pieter Isaacsz, 1612.*

31

THE GOVERNMENT & HISTORY OF DENMARK

ABOVE: *Frederik VII by August Schiøtt.*

EUROPEAN COUNTRIES TODAY: DENMARK

did suffer an economic decline as many of its most important trading partners were embroiled in the conflict.

By 1924, socialism had become a prominent force in Denmark's political life, and in that year the Social Democrats became the nation's largest political party, a distinction they retained until 2001. During the Great Depression of the 1930s, the Social Democrats worked with local businesspeople to overcome some of the economic difficulties of the period, which also helped the party to gain more mainstream acceptance. Much of the legislation that laid the foundation for the modern welfare state present in Denmark today was passed during this period.

World War II

By 1933, Adolph Hitler had come to power in nearby Germany, and by 1938 he had occupied neighboring Austria as well. His stated objective was to unify all ethnic German peoples. He soon demanded the surrender of Czechoslovakia's Sudetenland, taking up the cause of the Sudeten Germans. On September 29, 1938, France, Germany, Italy, and Great Britain signed the Munich Agreement, demanding that Czechoslovakia surrender the Sudetenland to Germany in exchange for a promise of peace. However, in March 1939, Hitler reneged on his agreement and invaded the remainder of Czechoslovakia. When it became clear that Hitler's aggression could not be stopped through negotiation and diplomacy, other nations had little choice but to declare war. Soon, much of the world was drawn in to the conflict.

Denmark once again proclaimed its neutrality, just as it had during World War I, but this time it could not evade involvement in the war. As the country shared a border with northern Germany, Hitler could not let it evade his control. On April 9, 1940, German forces invaded Denmark. Although thirty-nine Danish soldiers died during the invasion, the government ordered a halt to all resistance very early on, hoping to negotiate generous terms for the occupation. This approach was successful, as a cooperative Danish government meant that the Germans did not have to allocate manpower to oversee the daily affairs of the Danes.

THE GOVERNMENT & HISTORY OF DENMARK

ABOVE: *Ruins of an Atlantic Wall bunker at Lokken, built by the German armed forces during World War II.*

EUROPEAN COUNTRIES TODAY: DENMARK

In terms of Nazi race ideology, the Danes were considered to be fellow Aryans; the Nazis therefore considered the Danes more trustworthy than the Poles and the Slavs who inhabited other Nazi-occupied territories. As a result, the Danes were allowed to retain their democratically elected government, and many areas of life were largely unaffected by the occupation. Because relations with the Danes were so good, Nazi officials did not impose restrictions on Danish Jews like those imposed on other areas as they feared a backlash from the general population. However, as the occupation continued, many Danes became disenchanted with Nazi control and an armed resistance movement formed.

Episodes of resistance, both in the form of violent acts of sabotage and in nonviolent civil disturbances, increased to the point that the Nazis dissolved the Danish government. In August 1943, martial law was implemented. Shortly afterward, resistance workers learned of a plan to remove all Danish Jews to concentration camps in Czechoslovakia. Thousands of everyday Danish citizens worked together to smuggle their Jewish neighbors out of the country in advance of the Nazi operation.

Fishermen built secret compartments in their boats to hide Jews on the short trip to neutral Sweden. Small children and the sick and infirm who could not make the journey were given Danish names and hidden in orphanages and senior-citizen homes. Nazi soldiers began to suspect what was happening and used police dogs trained to find hidden people. To throw the dogs off, chemists in Sweden concocted a mixture of dried rabbit's blood and cocaine, placing it on handkerchiefs. These were distributed to the fishermen. When a dog detected the presence of the rabbit's blood, he would sniff the handkerchief, and the cocaine would temporarily disable its sense of smell.

Of the nation's estimated 8,000 Jews, only 450 were captured by the Nazis and sent to concentration camps. Of those, 51 died before the war's end. The swift action on the part of the Danish people no doubt saved thousands of lives. Historians have called the event "the largest episode of mass altruism in history."

Denmark was eventually liberated from Nazi occupation in 1945. Although Denmark was spared many of the horrors of the conflict, there was still a significant loss of life, and the years immediately following the war were marked by economic hardship.

THE GOVERNMENT & HISTORY OF DENMARK

Postwar Developments and the Denmark of Today

The years following World War II saw further political reform in Denmark. With the signing of a new constitution, the *Landsting* (the elected upper house of parliament) was abolished, and the female right of succession to the throne was guaranteed.

After the war, with the perceived threat posed by the Soviet Union and the lessons of World War II still fresh in Danish minds, the country abandoned its policy of neutrality. Denmark subsequently became a charter member of the United Nations and was one of the founding members of the North Atlantic Treaty Organisation (NATO). Denmark had originally tried to form a defense

Nordic Council

The Nordic Council is the official body for formal inter-parliamentary cooperation between the Nordic countries. It was formed in 1952 after the World War II to promote collaboration between the five Nordic countries. Its first concrete result was the introduction in 1952 of a common labor market and free movement across borders without passports for the countries' citizens.

The Council consists of 87 representatives from Denmark, Finland, Iceland, Norway, and Sweden, as well as the autonomous areas of the Faroe Islands, Greenland, and the Åland Islands. The Council holds ordinary sessions each year in October/November and usually one extra session per year with a specific theme. Since 1991 Estonia, Latvia, and Lithuania participate with observer status, as well as the German state of Schleswig-Holstein since 2016.

EUROPEAN COUNTRIES TODAY: DENMARK

ABOVE: Crown Princess Mary and Crown Prince Frederick.

THE GOVERNMENT & HISTORY OF DENMARK

ABOVE: Danish Royal Life Guards at Amalienborg Palace, Copenhagen. The palace is the official residence of Queen Margrethe II.

EUROPEAN COUNTRIES TODAY: DENMARK

alliance only with Norway and Sweden. As a result, the Nordic Council was later set up to coordinate policy between the three Nordic countries. In 1973, Danes voted yes to joining the European Community, the predecessor of the EU. Since then, Denmark has been a reluctant member of the European Community, opting out of many proposals, including the adoption of the euro as the national currency, which was rejected in a referendum in 2000. By 2007, however, many Danish leaders favored adopting the currency, but the decision was put off due the economic crisis that began in 2008. Since 2011, polls have consistently shown majority opposition to joining the Eurozone.

In the twenty-first century, Denmark has participated in major military and humanitarian operations, most notably the UN- and NATO-led operations in Cyprus, Bosnia and Herzegovina, Korea, Egypt, Croatia, Kosovo, Ethiopia, Iraq, Afghanistan, and Somalia. For such a small country, Denmark continues to play a very large role in the world!

Text-Dependent Questions

1. What are the Jelling Stones?

2. Who was Harald Bluetooth's father?

3. When did the Germans invade Denmark during World War II?

Research Project

Write a brief report on the Viking era in Denmark.

THE GOVERNMENT & HISTORY OF DENMARK

The Formation of the European Union (EU)

The EU is a confederation of European nations that continues to grow. As of 2017, there are twenty-eight official members. Several other candidates are also waiting for approval. All countries that enter the EU agree to follow common laws about foreign security policies. They also agree to cooperate on legal matters that go on within the EU. The European Council meets to discuss all international matters and make decisions about them. Each country's own concerns and interests are important, though. And apart from legal and financial issues, the EU tries to uphold values such as peace, human dignity, freedom, and equality.

All member countries remain autonomous. This means that they generally keep their own laws and regulations. The idea for a union among European nations was first mentioned after World War II. The war had devastated much of Europe, both physically and financially. In 1950, the French foreign minister suggested that France and West Germany combine their coal and steel industries under one authority. Both countries would have control over the

ABOVE: *The entrance to the European Union Parliament Building in Brussels.*

EUROPEAN COUNTRIES TODAY: DENMARK

Member Countries

Austria	Greece	Romania
Belgium	Hungary	Slovakia
Bulgaria	Ireland	Slovenia
Croatia	Italy	Spain
Cyprus	Latvia	Sweden
Czech Republic	Lithuania	United Kingdom
Denmark	Luxembourg	*(Brexit: For the time*
Estonia	Malta	*being, the United*
Finland	Netherlands	*Kingdom remains a full*
France	Poland	*member of the EU.)*
Germany	Portugal	

industries. This would help them become more financially stable. It would also make war between the countries much more difficult. The idea was interesting to other European countries as well. In 1951, France, West Germany, Belgium, Luxembourg, the Netherlands, and Italy signed the Treaty of Paris, creating the European Coal and Steel Community. These six countries would become the core of the EU.

In 1957, these same countries signed the Treaties of Rome, creating the European Economic Community. In 1965, the Merger Treaty formed the European Community. Finally, in 1992, the Maastricht Treaty was signed. This treaty defined the European Union. It gave a framework for expanding the EU's political role, particularly in the area of foreign and security policy. It would also replace national currencies with the euro. The next year, the treaty went into effect. At that time, the member countries included the original six plus another six who had joined during the 1970s and '80s.

In the following years, the EU would take more steps to form a single market for its members. This would make joining the union even more advantageous. In addition to enlargement, the EU is steadily becoming more integrated through its own policies for closer cooperation between member states.

Words to Understand

domestic: Relating to or originating within a country.

geothermal: Relating to or utilizing the heat of the earth's interior.

progressive: Making use of new ideas, findings, or opportunities.

BELOW: Fishing boats moored to the quay at Elsinore (Helsingør) harbor. While the overall contribution of the fisheries sector to the country's economy is only about 0.5 percent, Denmark is ranked fifth in the world in exports of fish and fish products. Approximately 20,000 Danish people are employed in fishing, aquaculture, and related industries.

Chapter Three
THE DANISH ECONOMY

Denmark is able to maintain its high standard of living due to the relative strength of its economy. Although recent economic downturns in other parts of Europe have affected the Danish economy, the country has still maintained a small margin of economic growth. The nation's well-developed infrastructure, highly educated and well-paid workforce, and **progressive** energy policies have all helped to develop the strong market economy that thrives in Denmark today.

ABOVE: *Esbjerg Port on the southwest coast of Jutland has been transformed from a fishing and ferry harbor to a major Nordic intermodal hub with the largest handling of wind turbine cargo in Europe. It is also a major center for repairing oil rigs.*

THE DANISH ECONOMY

The New Economy

As is happening in many industrialized nations, Denmark has made a shift away from manufacturing as the primary source of economic growth. Although nearly one-third of Denmark's gross domestic product (GDP) still comes from its manufacturing enterprises, the dominant source of Denmark's income today comes from the service sector, which contributes 69 percent of the country's GDP. This includes the country's robust shipping industry and the emerging sectors of information technology and tourism.

ABOVE: *The old Carlsberg Brewery in Valby, Copenhagen is now a museum. You can find out about the beer making process, explore the old buildings, taste the world-famous Danish beers in many styles, and generally get to know about the industry.*

EUROPEAN COUNTRIES TODAY: DENMARK

Danish Beer

Beer production in Denmark is dominated by Carlsberg, who also own the famous brand, Tuborg. The Danish market is dominated by pale lager, with more than 95 percent of total sales. However, stout and other dark beers are increasing in popularity, a trend driven by the market growth of premium-priced beers. A number of regional breweries produce beer on a smaller scale. Microbreweries are also getting more popular, and produce a wide variety of beer styles. Imported beer accounts for a tiny percentage of consumption.

Industry

Denmark has a developed industrial economy. Despite the country's small size, the manufacturing sector in Denmark is very diverse and produces a variety of high-quality goods, both for export and for domestic consumption. Meat-processing factories, cigarette factories, dairies, corn mills, and breweries are among the most important industries of the food, beverage, and tobacco industries. Petroleum, insulin, and plastic goods are the main products produced by the Danish chemical industry.

From the nation's booming mechanical engineering industry come motors, agricultural machines, pumps, thermostats, refrigerators, and telecommunications equipment. Finally, furniture, clothing, and toys are among the Danish industrial products sold in the greatest numbers. Major structural changes among the different areas of trade have brought new developments within the manufacturing sector. The manufacture of mechanical engineering products, which also includes electronic goods, represents a growing proportion of the sector's productive value. The same applies to the chemical industry.

In contrast, the food, beverage, and tobacco industries have had a more or less constant share of production, whereas the textile, clothing, and leather

THE DANISH ECONOMY

industries have clearly been in decline. This can be attributed to increased competition from third world countries and, more recently, the new EU member countries of Central and Eastern Europe, who can produce similar goods much less expensively due to the greater availability of raw materials and cheap labor.

Agriculture

Danish agriculture produces enough food each year to feed 15 million people, which is almost three times the tiny nation's total population. Although the importance of agriculture in the Danish economy overall has fallen steadily with the rise of industrialization and the tremendous growth of the services sector, it is still an essential occupation due to its effect on employment and its importance in supplying everyday foodstuffs. As agricultural land accounts for almost two-thirds of the total area of the country, the industry is also important because of its impact on both the cultural and the scenic landscapes.

ABOVE: A Lego model of a Royal Life Guard in the Lego store in Copenhagen. The plastic bricks are one of Denmark's most famous exports.

    Farming in Denmark today is largely governed by the agricultural policies laid down by the EU, whose member countries are guaranteed a sale price for their agricultural goods that is better than that of the world market, regardless of whether sales are to the **domestic** market, the EU, or to markets outside the EU. The support Danish farmers receive from the EU has helped make Denmark one of the most sophisticated agricultural regions in the whole world. Farming methods in Denmark have been developed and implemented to prevent negative environmental impacts, decrease the use of pesticides, conserve energy, and most importantly, provide the end consumer with a safe

EUROPEAN COUNTRIES TODAY: DENMARK

ABOVE: A modern farm on the island of Møn.

THE DANISH ECONOMY

and wholesome food supply. As a result, Denmark has benefited greatly from EU agricultural policies.

Energy

Denmark's holdings in the North Sea produce more oil and natural gas than is needed domestically. This has resulted in energy becoming a vital export. Oil and gas are taken ashore, then distributed and exported via pipelines. Gas is exported to Sweden and Germany, while the surplus oil is sold to a variety of countries. Denmark is the third-largest oil producer in Western Europe after Norway and Great Britain. Together with gas production, the nation's oil wealth is an important reason why Denmark has had an energy surplus for the last two decades.

ABOVE: *The covered food market at Torvehallerne, Copenhagen is famous for its stands selling everything from fish and meat to gourmet delicacies and exotic spices.*

EUROPEAN COUNTRIES TODAY: DENMARK

The Economy of Denmark

Gross Domestic Product (GDP): $275.3 billion (2016 est.)
GDP Per Capita: $46,600 (2016 est.)
Industries: Iron, steel, nonferrous metals, chemicals, food processing, machinery and transportaion equipment, textiles and clothing, electronics, construction, furniture and other wood products, shipbuilding and refurbishments, medical equipment
Agriculture: barley, wheat, potatoes, sugar beet, pork, dairy products, fish
Export Commodities: machinery and instruments, meat and meat products, dairy products, fish, pharmaceuticals, furniture and design, wind turbines
Export Partners: Germany 15.1%, Sweden 11.4%, Norway 6.2%, UK 6%, US 5%, Netherlands 4.5%, China 4.2% (2016)
Import Commodities: machinery and equipment, raw materials, chemicals, grain and foodstuffs, consumer goods
Import Partners: Germany 21.4%, Sweden 12.3%, Netherlands 8%, China 7.6%, UK 4.2%, Norway 4.2% (2016)
Currency: Danish krone

Source: www.cia.gov 2017

Electricity is mainly produced in regional power stations by burning coal supplemented with natural gas, oil, biological fuel, and waste products. Natural gas is playing an increasingly important role, while the use of oil is decreasing. Most heating energy is currently produced in the home. Technology used in homes and offices for heating include oil and gas boilers, straw- and wood-burning stoves, solar energy, ground heat, and **geothermal** heating systems. Until recently, oil-burning furnaces in individual homes were the traditional

49

THE DANISH ECONOMY

ABOVE: *Avedøre Power Plant near Copenhagen is a high-technology facility, and one of the world's most efficient of its kind. It is able to utilize as much as 94 percent of the energy in the fuel when converting it into electricity. Apart from using coal, petroleum, and natural gas, the plant runs on a wide variety of biomass fuels, such as straw and wood pellets.*

EUROPEAN COUNTRIES TODAY: DENMARK

Educational Video

Denmark's Green Revolution leads the way in sustainable energy solutions.

ABOVE: Apartment living is very popular in Denmark. All new homes are well insulated and have good energy ratings.

51

THE DANISH ECONOMY

Danish form of heating, but their numbers are falling, and domestic heating is being replaced by other methods. Only in rural districts is oil included in heating plans for the future. Natural gas pipelines have been taken to most homes in the more densely populated areas. There is no obligation to be connected to the pipelines, but the Danish people have a strong sense that it is important to do one's part for the environment—so most families are making a switch.

Individual consumption of energy is much lower in Denmark than in most industrialized nations. Conservation of energy plays an important role in energy planning. A government program was introduced to promote the insulation of Danish homes; as a result, nearly all homes have now been insulated. A heating inspection is required when houses are sold. In addition, citizens are encouraged to conserve energy through grants and information campaigns.

ABOVE: *Cycling is a very popular mode of transport, particularly in the cities (such as Copenhagen).*

EUROPEAN COUNTRIES TODAY: DENMARK

Wind power is very important in Denmark. Today, wind power provides almost half of Denmark's total electricity generation requirement.

Transportation

Denmark has 44,669 miles (71,888 km) of road and 1,720 miles (2,768 km) of railway, 291 railway stations and goods terminals, 124 ports, and 23 airports. Most people travel by car in Denmark. In recent years, car and railway traffic has increased as more bridges have been built between Denmark's many islands, while ferry and domestic flight traffic has decreased. Most goods transported domestically are carried by Danish trucks, while most goods transported internationally are carried by ship. Only a limited number of exports are transported by train and very few by plane.

Text-Dependent Questions

1. Why is Denmark's economy relatively stable?

2. What kinds of products does Denmark produce?

3. Why are Danish homes so energy efficient?

Research Project

Write a report on the development of wind power in Denmark. Explain why the development of renewable energy is so important and why it is opposed in some instances.

Words to Understand

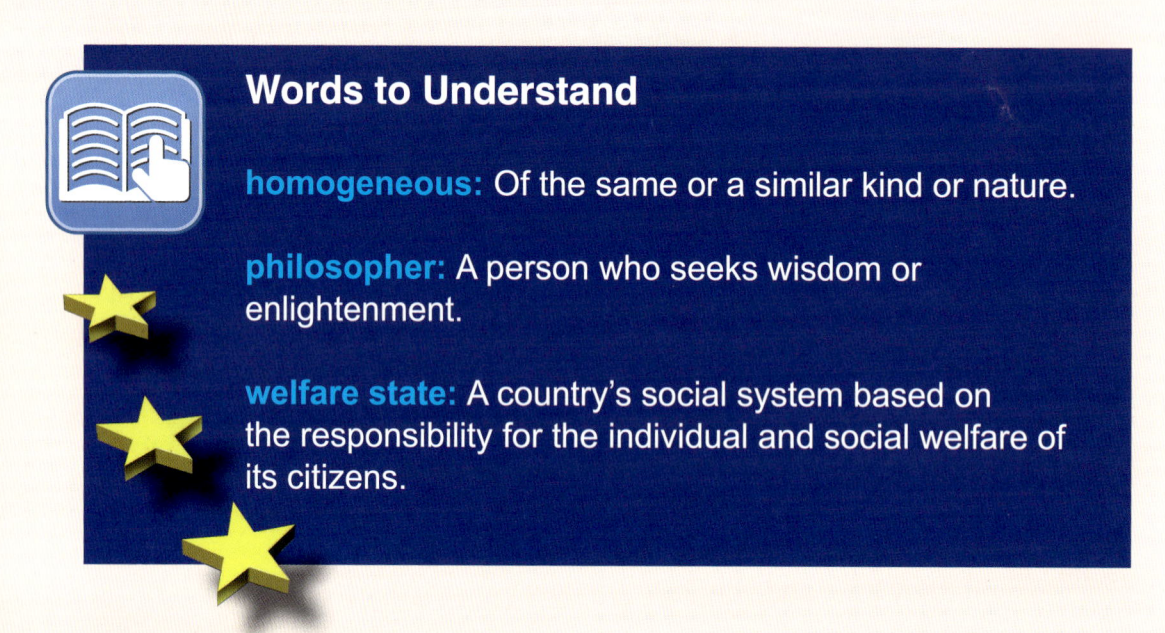

homogeneous: Of the same or a similar kind or nature.

philosopher: A person who seeks wisdom or enlightenment.

welfare state: A country's social system based on the responsibility for the individual and social welfare of its citizens.

BELOW: The Øresund Bridge links Copenhagen with Malmö in Sweden. It is nearly 5 miles (8 km) long. The bridge is very important for both countries, but particularly for Sweden as it links it with mainland Europe.

Chapter Four
CITIZENS OF DENMARK: PEOPLE, CUSTOMS & CULTURE

Denmark, home to more than 5 million people, is a small but vibrant country. Although the country's population includes 400,000 citizens of foreign origin, Denmark is generally considered to be ethnically and religiously **homogeneous**. Danish is the national language. An ancient language, it is related to both German and the old Viking tongue. Many Danish words are used in more than one way. For instance, *hej* means "hello," but *hej hej* means "goodbye." The pronunciation of Danish is difficult for nonnative speakers because the consonants are often barely enunciated, which makes them difficult for the untrained listener to detect.

ABOVE: *Danes have a relaxed view on marriage, with many not bothering with it at all.*

CITIZENS OF DENMARK: PEOPLE, CUSTOMS & CULTURE

ABOVE: This gay couple have just married, something which was legalized in Denmark in 2012.

The structure of the traditional Danish family has undergone some changes in the last few decades. Today, it is normal for a couple to live together for many years in what is known as a "paperless marriage." It is also considered normal for couples to have children without being wed, and many women keep their maiden names after they are married, which means that Danish children often inherit two last names. Same-sex marriage became legal in Denmark on June 15, 2012. The bill for legalization, introduced by the government of Helle Thorning-Schmidt, was approved by the Danish parliament on June 7, 2012 and received Royal Assent on June 12, 2012. Same-sex couples were previously recognized through registered partnerships. Denmark was the eleventh country in the world to legalize same-sex marriage.

EUROPEAN COUNTRIES TODAY: DENMARK

ABOVE: *During the winter, when the weather is bad, Danes enjoy socializing indoors amid food, candlelight, and a cozy atmosphere. The Danes call this hygge.*

CITIZENS OF DENMARK: PEOPLE, CUSTOMS & CULTURE

The Welfare State

Since the creation of the so-called **welfare state** in the 1970s, Denmark has boasted one of the highest standards of living in the world. Its programs include a highly developed social security system, which guarantees that no one will suffer a serious decline in their standard of living due to illness or unemployment. In addition, anyone aged sixty-seven or older is entitled to an old-age pension, and all citizens can access free health care. All Danish students have the right to a free education, including studies at the university level. Naturally, the cost of these programs is considerable, and the Danish people currently pay one of the highest levels of income tax in the world to finance these social programs.

Religion

All Danish citizens enjoy complete freedom of religion, and the law protects the right of citizens to worship freely. The official religion of Denmark is the Lutheranism, and nearly 90 percent of Danes are baptized into the Lutheran Evangelical Church. The second-largest religious faith in Denmark is Islam, owing to the large numbers of immigrants who have made their way to Denmark in recent decades from the Middle East and North Africa. A number of smaller Christian churches are represented in Denmark, and they have been accorded the status of officially recognized religious communities. These include the Roman Catholic Church, the Danish Baptist Church, the Pentecostal Church, the Seventh Day Adventists, the Catholic Apostolic Church, the Salvation Army, the Methodist Church, the Anglican Church, and the Russian Orthodox Church.

Education and Sports

Danes take both education and sports very seriously. Almost all adults can read and write, and most can speak at least one foreign language; many speak two. The country has produced great thinkers and sports figures.

Education is compulsory in Denmark. Virtually all children in attend public schools and all public schools are free. Less than 10 percent of Danish

EUROPEAN COUNTRIES TODAY: DENMARK

Educational Video

Education and healthcare in Denmark.

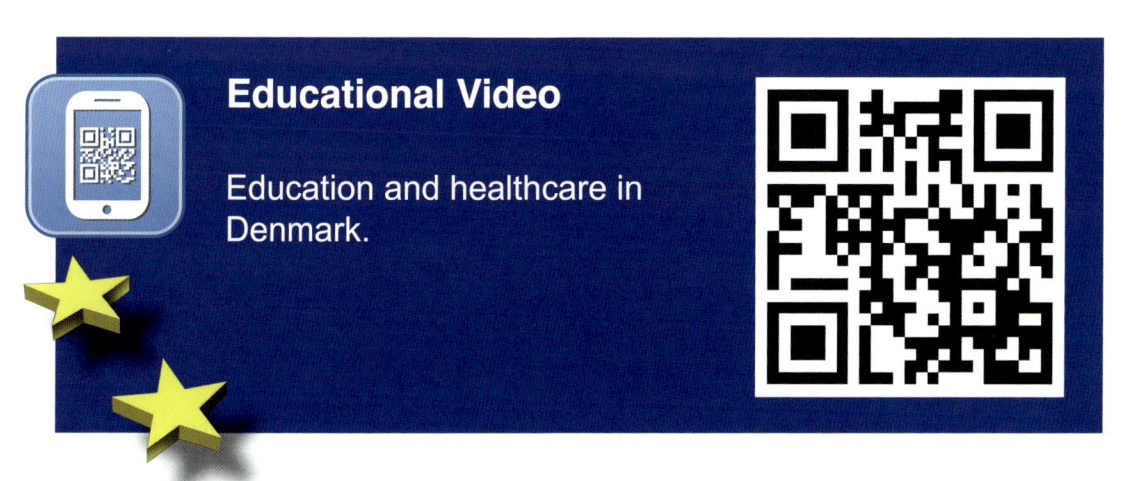

ABOVE: Copenhagen high school students celebrate their graduation day on the streets of the city.

CITIZENS OF DENMARK: PEOPLE, CUSTOMS & CULTURE

students choose to attend private schools, which require that private tuition be paid by a student's parents. Attending a college or university is also free in Denmark, with students receiving government grants on a monthly basis.

Soccer—or football, as it is known in Europe—is Denmark's national sport, but swimming, sailing, cycling, and cross-country running are also very popular, both as spectator sports and as pastimes for all citizens. A growing number of people now go jogging in the morning or evening. Denmark has won Olympic gold medals in handball, sailing, riding, shooting, swimming, rowing, tug-of-war, and cycling.

ABOVE: *Denmark vs. Romania in FIFA World Cup qualifier in 2017. Denmark are in red and white.*

EUROPEAN COUNTRIES TODAY: DENMARK

ABOVE: *Danish cyclist Lars Ytting Bak of Lotto Soudal Team riding during a time trial in the professional Paris-Nice cycling race in France.*

CITIZENS OF DENMARK: PEOPLE, CUSTOMS & CULTURE

Food and Drink

The heart of the Danish diet does not lie with any one particular dish but rather in the whole idea and presentation of the cold buffet. The basic elements are bread, cold meat, fish, or cheese, and the condiments placed on top of other items. Not just any combination will do, however. Certain meats and cheeses are used exclusively with certain breads. The bread is either rye or white and is always eaten buttered. The most common sandwiches are: smoked herring topped with egg yolk, radishes, and chives; smoked eel with scrambled eggs; pork with red cabbage, apples, and prunes; or liverwurst with pickles. The most common way for Danes to eat lunch is from a madpakken (lunch box), where open-faced sandwiches specially wrapped in wax paper are consumed. Thus, lunch is available at work or school with a minimum of fuss.

ABOVE: *Noma is a Michelin two-star restaurant run by chef René Redzepi in Copenhagen. The restaurant is known for its reinvention and interpretation of the Nordic cuisine. It has been ranked best restaurant in the world a number of times by the restaurant press.*

EUROPEAN COUNTRIES TODAY: DENMARK

Frikadeller
(Danish Meatballs)

Makes 4 servings

Ingredients
1 pound of pork and beef mixed (half and half)
4 tablespoons of flour
1 whole egg
1 medium grated onion
½ a cup of milk
salt and pepper to taste
oil for frying

Directions
Mix all the ingredients together in a large bowl. Shape into four balls and flatten slightly. Heat the oil in a large pan and fry the balls until they are thoroughly cooked through. Serve with fries or mashed potato, vegetables, or salad.

Mandelsmørboller
(Almond Butter Balls)

Makes 6–8 servings

Ingredients
1 cup of soft butter
3 tablespoons of powdered sugar
1 teaspoon of vanilla extract
¼ teaspoon of almond extract
1½ cups of sifted flour
1 cup of finely chopped almonds
additional powdered sugar and flaked almonds to decorate

Directions
Cream the butter and sugar. Add extracts and mix well. Stir in flour and fold in the chopped almonds. Roll into 6–8 balls and place on an ungreased cookie sheet. Bake at 350°F for 20 minutes. Roll warm cookies in powdered sugar and decorate with almonds.

CITIZENS OF DENMARK: PEOPLE, CUSTOMS & CULTURE

Denmark: A Proud Nation

Denmark's red and white flag is the Dannebrog, "flag of the Danes." Legend has it that the Dannebrog was seen as God's way of inspiring the Danish forces during a particularly bloody battle in the sky on June 15, 1219 (see page 8).

Danes fly their flag with pride. People in rural areas often have their own flagpole set squarely in the middle of their garden. On holidays and birthdays, miniature flags are used as table decorations, and Christmas trees are traditionally trimmed with miniature versions of the flag. Use of the Danish flag has also become important in advertising and promoting domestically produced products in the marketplace. Danish soccer fans are proud of the fact that they were the first fans to paint their faces and bodies with their flag in support of the national soccer team. Unlike the displays sometimes seen in other countries, to display the flag in Denmark is not a sign of nationalism but rather a long-standing cultural custom.

ABOVE: *Danish soccer fans were the first to paint their faces when supporting a national team.*

EUROPEAN COUNTRIES TODAY: DENMARK

Famous Danes

Danish society has produced many important thinkers, artists, and scientists. Danes are very proud of the contributions made by some of their famous citizens.

Hans Christian Andersen, born in Odense on the island of Funen to a shoemaker and a washerwoman, wrote fanciful fairy tales that have been a source of delight to children and adults throughout the world. A statue of the Little Mermaid, perhaps Andersen's most beloved character, is now one of Copenhagen's biggest tourist attractions.

ABOVE: Niels Bohr.

ABOVE: Søren Kierkegaard.

ABOVE: Karen Blixen.

BELOW: Hans Christian Andersen's house and museum.

ABOVE: Hans Christian Andersen.

Hans Christian Andersen (1805–75)

Hans Christian Andersen was a Danish author. Although a prolific writer of plays, travelogues, novels, and poems, Andersen is best remembered for his fairy tales. Andersen's popularity is not limited to children; his fantastic tales, called *eventyr* in Danish, express themes that transcend age and nationality. Andersen's fairy tales, of which there are no fewer than 3,381 works translated into more than 125 languages, have become culturally embedded in the West's collective consciousness. Readily accessible to children, but presenting lessons of virtue and resilience in the face of adversity, his stories are for mature readers as well. Some of his most famous fairy tales include "The Emperor's New Clothes," "The Little Mermaid," "The Nightingale," "The Snow Queen," "The Ugly Duckling," "Thumbelina," and many others. His stories have inspired ballets, plays, and animated and live-action films.

ABOVE: *The historic quarter of Odense, where Hans Christian Andersen was born, is now an open-air museum.*

🇩🇰 CITIZENS OF DENMARK: PEOPLE, CUSTOMS & CULTURE

ABOVE: Karen Blixen's house in Kenya insipred her to write Out of Africa.

EUROPEAN COUNTRIES TODAY: DENMARK

Søren Kierkegaard was also a famous writer, although his subject matter was a little more serious. A notable **philosopher**, Kierkegaard wrote many books on Christianity and the philosophical problems of modern existence.

Author Karen Blixen invented the pseudonym Isak Dinesen and went on to use it for most of her writing career. For many years she lived in Kenya, where her most famous novel, *Out of Africa*, was written. Today, tourists can visit both the farm she lived on in Kenya and her house in Rungsted, Denmark.

The nation has also produced great scientists, including the famous Nobel Prize-winning physicist Niels Bohr. Bohr was one of the fathers of atomic energy and also helped to organize the periodic table. A brilliant researcher and one of the most prominent personalities in modern science, he was also very outspoken about the consequences and ethical implications of the invention of the nuclear bomb.

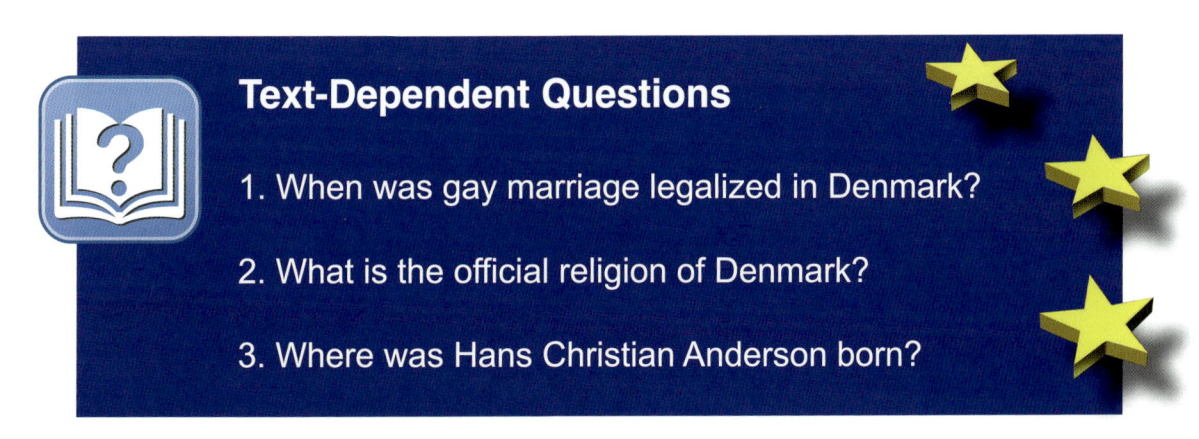

Text-Dependent Questions

1. When was gay marriage legalized in Denmark?

2. What is the official religion of Denmark?

3. Where was Hans Christian Anderson born?

Research Project

Write a brief report on famous Danes.

Words to Understand

environment: The circumstances, objects, or conditions by which one is surrounded.

metropolitan: Relating to a large city and its surrounding suburbs.

symphony: An instrumental piece of music, often in several movements.

BELOW: Tivoli Gardens is situated in the center of Copenhagen. It is one of the world's oldest theme parks and is famous for its rides, attractions, performances, and cultural activities for both adults and children alike.

Chapter Five
THE FAMOUS CITIES OF DENMARK

Today's Denmark is a highly urban society. Eighty-five percent of all Danes live in towns. The **metropolitan** Copenhagen region is home to nearly two million people. The second-largest city is Aarhus, with a population of about 240,000. In addition, a network of medium-sized towns connected by modern highways and bridges covers the entire country.

Copenhagen

Copenhagen is Denmark's capital and most populated city. From its origins as a humble fishing village to its current status as the nation's capital, Copenhagen offers visitors more than a thousand years of history and culture in the carefully preserved monuments and architecture of this beautiful city. Denmark is home to Europe's oldest continuous monarchy, and all over the city there are breathtaking monuments and exquisite royal palaces to educate and excite the thousands of tourists who make their way to Copenhagen from all over the world.

As the nation's capital, the city is also the center of the Danish government, as well as a hub for

ABOVE: *The Church of St. Nicholas, Copenhagen.*

THE FAMOUS CITIES OF DENMARK

Educational Video

Travel to Denmark. Two perfect days in Copenhagen with Ralph Grizzle.

ABOVE: Nyhavn (New Harbor) is a waterfront, canal, and entertainment district in Copenhagen. It is lined with brightly colored seventeenth- and early eighteenth-century town houses. Nyhavn is known for its bars, cafes, restaurants, and the historic wooden ships that are moored in the harbor.

EUROPEAN COUNTRIES TODAY: DENMARK

ABOVE: *Amalienborg is the official residence of the Danish royal family. It consists of four identical classical palace facades with rococo interiors. Every day, visitors can experience the changing of the guards as they march from their barracks by Rosenborg Castle through the streets of Copenhagen. The changing of the guard takes place at 12:00 noon.*

transportation, industry, and education. It has a long and distinguished cultural history, and events hosted in Copenhagen annually include the Viking Pageant, the Copenhagen Jazz Festival, and the Roskilde Festival, known internationally as Europe's largest party, featuring four days of concerts with artists from genres as varied as rock, pop, soul, R & B, electronic, and hip-hop.

THE FAMOUS CITIES OF DENMARK

The Little Mermaid

The Little Mermaid is a bronze statue by Edvard Eriksen, depicting the character from Hans Christian Andersen's famous book. The sculpture is displayed on a rock by the waterside at the Langelinie promenade in Copenhagen. The statue was commissioned in 1909 by Carl Jacobsen, son of the founder of the Carlsberg Brewery. She was unveiled in 1913. The Little Mermaid is a Copenhagen icon, and receives more than a million visitors a year. The Little Mermaid is also the most photographed statue in Denmark.

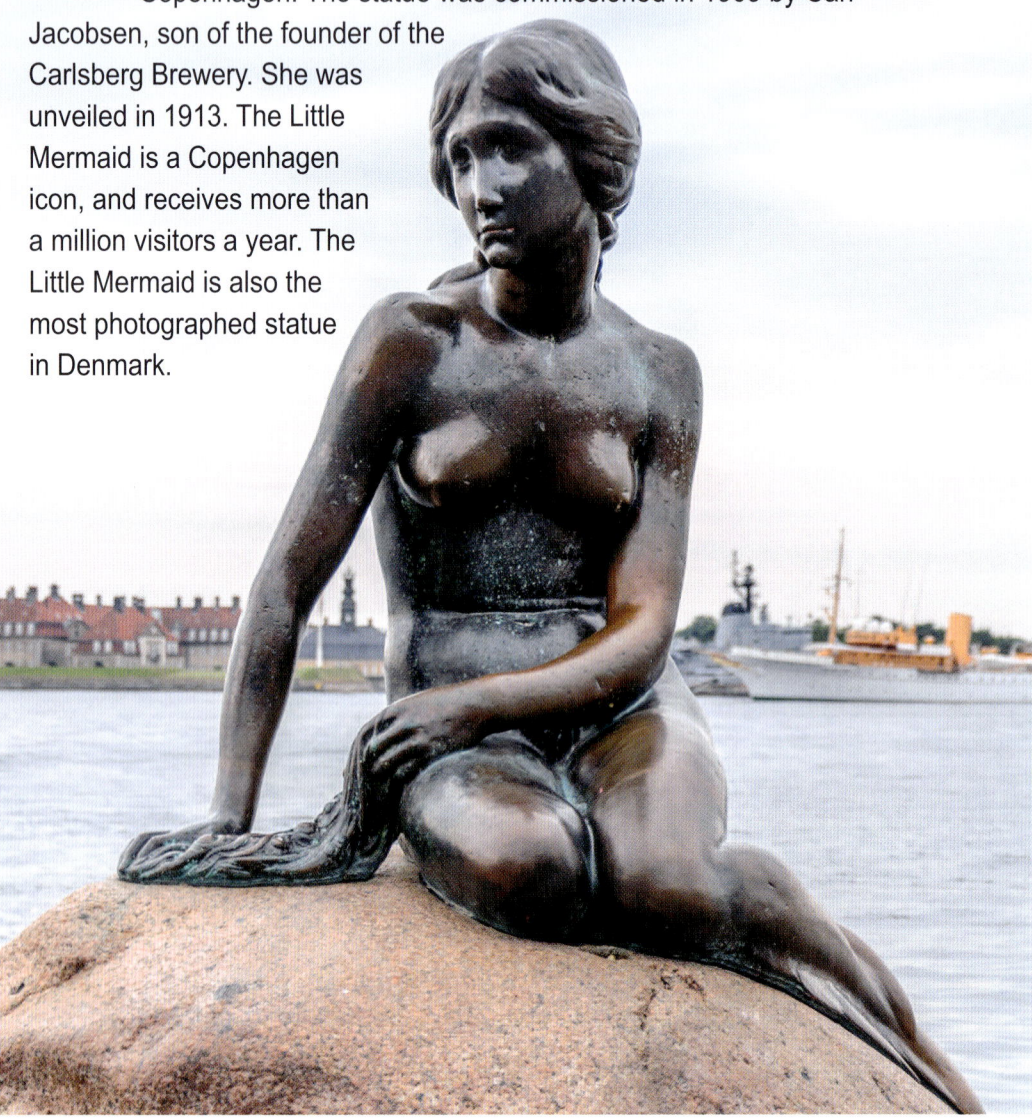

EUROPEAN COUNTRIES TODAY: DENMARK

Aarhus

Denmark's second-most populated city, Aarhus, has been continually inhabited since Viking times. The original city grew up around the mouth of the Aarhus River. Vikings decided to settle on this spot because of the location's excellent potential as a harbor and trading post. The Danish word for "river mouth" was at that time *arus*, and this is the word from which the city's name originates.

Aarhus has an active business community and a vibrant educational **environment** with many colleges and universities. As a result, the city is home

ABOVE: A new residential complex called Isbjerget *(The Iceberg) in Aarhus. It is part of the newly regenerated harbor area.*

75

THE FAMOUS CITIES OF DENMARK

ABOVE: *People enjoying a sunny day at the promenade by the river in Aarhus, which is Denmark's second largest city.*

to thousands of young people, contributing to the cultural life of the city and its continued growth. The city has a wealth of excellent restaurants, a unique café environment, and a host of musical offerings with the Concert Hall, the Aarhus Symphony Orchestra, and the Danish National Opera among the city's many musical venues.

EUROPEAN COUNTRIES TODAY: DENMARK

The Old Town, Aarhus

The Old Town in Aarhus (Den Gamle By), is an open-air town museum located in the Aarhus Botanical Gardens. The museum was opened in 1914 as the world's first open-air museum of its kind, concentrating on the culture and architecture of Danish towns. Today, the museum is one of a few top-rated Danish museums outside Copenhagen, serving more than 400,000 visitors each year. The museum consists of seventy-five historical buildings relocated from towns in all parts of the country. The architecture of the town itself is the main attraction; however, most of the buildings are open for visitors. The interiors are either decorated in the original historical style or are home to larger exhibits. There are shops, cafés, a school, a theater, and workshops in the town. The museum houses an interesting collection of clocks and watches, as well as silverware and delftware at the Gallery of Decorative Arts.

THE FAMOUS CITIES OF DENMARK

Odense

Odense, the third-largest city in Denmark, is the capital of the island of Funen. Odense is one of the oldest cities in Denmark and celebrated its one-thousandth anniversary as a city in 1998. The famous author and poet Hans Christian Anderson was born here on April 2, 1805. A house in the oldest part of Odense has been turned into a museum dedicated to him and holds a large collection of his works and belongings, and his childhood home is a museum as well. The city also features a museum honoring the classical composer Carl Nielsen, who was born nearby.

More recently, Odense has gained prominence as an industrial center. Many important Danish industries are headquartered here. These include Denmark's biggest shipyard, Odense Steel Shipyard, as well as the site of the country's largest wholesale auction of vegetables, fruits, and flowers, and the Albani Brewery, which brews the locally brewed beer, Odense Pilsner. The city also has several important cultural attractions, including a Gothic cathedral, a theater, a **symphony** orchestra, a zoo, and the Funen Village, an open-air museum featuring historical houses that were moved there from the Funen region.

ABOVE: Odense Town Hall at Christmas.

EUROPEAN COUNTRIES TODAY: DENMARK

ABOVE: *A cobbled street in Odense.*

Text Dependent Questions

1. Where is the Danish government located?

2. Where is the Danish National Opera situated?

3. Where was Carl Nielsen born?

Research Project

Write a one-page biography on Carl Nielsen, the Danish composer.

Words to Understand

commuters: People who travel between home and work.

embargo: An order of a government prohibiting the departure of commercial ships from its ports.

gastronomy: The art or science of good eating.

BELOW: This modern Danish eco-home is a "passive house" which means it is built to the highest energy-saving standards.

Chapter Six
A BRIGHT FUTURE FOR DENMARK

Like the rest of the world, Denmark has many problems to solve. Immigration issues, terrorism, financial crises, prejudice, and political conflicts are challenges that face most of the world's countries, and Denmark is no exception.

What Denmark has going for it is a well-educated population who possess many resources. Hopefully, these strengths will allow the Danes to find ways to overcome their challenges and emerge even stronger in the future.

Environmental Advancements

One of Denmark's greatest strengths is the way it is protecting the environment for the future. Denmark was one of the world's first nations to wake up to the dangers of foreign oil dependence after the 1973 Arab oil **embargo**. At that time, oil (almost all of it imported) met 90 percent of the country's energy needs. Denmark's leaders responded by putting their nation on a path toward energy independence.

New homes in Denmark today are twice as energy efficient as they

ABOVE: *EU and Danish flags.*

A BRIGHT FUTURE FOR DENMARK

ABOVE: *Despite joining the European Union, Denmark has kept its own currency, the Danish krone. Sweden and the UK are two other member countries that have not adopted the euro.*

were before the oil embargo. What's more, waste heat from local power plants heats Denmark's homes and offices. Denmark's taxes on new cars and motor fuel are among the highest in Europe, which has encouraged Danes to find other ways to get around. In Copenhagen, a third of **commuters** travel by bike. The average Dane uses less than half as much energy each year as the average American!

Denmark is also committed to wind energy. Since 1979, the Danish government has supported wind farms, and today Denmark gets 20 percent of its electricity from wind energy. The country's wind industry employs about 26,000 people, nearly 1 percent of the workforce, and wind energy accounts for 7 percent of Denmark's export income. Government leaders and utility executives expect wind to provide fully half of the country's electricity by the 2020s. To reach this goal, Denmark is looking to new offshore wind projects.

EUROPEAN COUNTRIES TODAY: DENMARK

Danish Economy

Denmark is experiencing a modest economic expansion. The economy grew by 1.6 percent in 2015 and an estimated 1.3 percent in 2016. The expansion is expected to continue at similar rates in 2017 and 2018. The labor market has strengthened since 2013, and unemployment stood at 4.2 percent in early 2017, based on the national measure. By early 2017, some sectors were experiencing difficulties attracting qualified labor. Productivity growth was significantly below the OECD average from the mid-1990s until 2011, but has increased in recent years. Improvement in productivity is needed to ensure continued growth. Denmark had a budget deficit of 1.4 percent in 2016. The government projects lower deficits in 2017 and 2018, and public debt as a share of GDP is expected to decline. In 2015, household indebtedness remained relatively high at more than 292 percent of net disposable income, while household net worth— from private pension schemes and other assets—amounted to 497 percent of net disposable income.

Source www.cia.gov 2017

ABOVE: Copenhagen's financial district.

🇩🇰 A BRIGHT FUTURE FOR DENMARK

ABOVE: Vertical axis wind turbines generate renewable, sustainable, and alternative energy in the Baltic Sea off the coast of Denmark.

EUROPEAN COUNTRIES TODAY: DENMARK

Even cars will soon be able to plug into this totally clean source of power, recharging during low-demand nighttime hours when Denmark's winds continue to blow.

Tourism in Denmark

Tourism in Denmark constitutes a growth industry. Every year millions of tourists visit the country. Some come to see attractions such as Tivoli, the Little Mermaid, or Legoland. Others come to enjoy Danish food culture and the New Nordic Cuisine that today dominates the world of **gastronomy**. And some come

ABOVE: *Many commuters, students, and tourists prefer using bicyles instead of cars or buses to move around the city.*

A BRIGHT FUTURE FOR DENMARK

to enjoy the Danish countryside with its many thousands of miles of coastline. Biking is very popular in Denmark, which has many established cycling routes. Swimming, windsurfing, yachting, and fishing are other outdoor opportunities to enjoy. Denmark has long stretches of sandy beaches, attract many tourists in the summer, with Germany accounting for most foreign visitors. Swedish and Norwegian tourists often come to visit the relatively lively city of Copenhagen, while many young Scandinavians come for Denmark's comparably cheap and readily accessible beer, wines, and spirits.

As Europe's oldest kingdom and the home of Hans Christian Andersen, Denmark is often marketed as a fairytale country. However, it is not just the obvious attractions that visitors flock to in Denmark. Other attractions include its fascinating zoos, museums, historical parks, and art galleries.

ABOVE: *Denmark has mile upon mile of beautiful unspolit sandy beaches, perfect for swimming and water sports when the weather is good.*

EUROPEAN COUNTRIES TODAY: DENMARK

ABOVE: Copenhagen's tourism industry is doing very well. Travelers from other European countries make use of low-cost airlines for weekends away.

🇩🇰 A BRIGHT FUTURE FOR DENMARK

ABOVE: *Denmark's pharmaceutical industries are important to its economy. The country is a major manufacturer of the drug insulin, used for the treatment of diabetes.*

Christiania is another unique and interesting place to visit. More than a city district of Copenhagen, Christiania is a way of life that started as an idealistic social experiment and has survived and adapted through the decades.

Denmark and the United States

Denmark's relationship with the United States has been good for a long time. These two countries have worked together for decades, and the United States is currently Denmark's largest trade partner outside of Europe. American culture has had a strong influence on Denmark, especially when it comes to music and television. Many tourists from the United States find their way to Denmark throughout the year.

EUROPEAN COUNTRIES TODAY: DENMARK

Denmark is home to many multinational pharmaceutical companies. Key products include diabetes care medications and devices. Danish companies are renowned for their research into growth hormone therapy and hormone replacement therapy.

As the world becomes more intimately connected, the relationship Denmark has with the United States will only continue to grow. Hopefully, America will be most inspired by Denmark's commitment to the environment. If the United States and countries around the globe can learn from Denmark's example, the world's future will be far brighter!

Text Dependent Questions

1. Why is biking popular in Denmark?

2. What outdoor activities are popular with tourists?

3. Why is Copenhagen a popular destination for young Scandinavians?

Research Project

Write a brief report on New Nordic Cuisine.

CHRONOLOGY

3000 BCE	Denmark's earliest inhabitants settle along the coast.
500 CE	The Danes invade from neighboring Sweden and conquer it.
800	Godfred the Viking establishes Denmark's boundaries and repels the Franks.
900	Gorm the Old establishes the Danish monarchy.
950	King Harald Bluetooth begins to convert Denmark to Christianity.
1448	King of Denmark Christian I ascends to the throne.
1660	King Frederik III decrees a hereditary monarchy for Denmark and Norway.
1848	Denmark's Liberal Party calls on King Frederik VII to renounce the system of absolute monarchy.
1849	The Danish Constitution is signed into law.
1914	World War I begins; Denmark remains neutral.
1915	Women are granted the right to vote.
1940	Nazi Germany invades Denmark.
1945	Denmark is liberated from Nazi occupation by the Allies.
1945	Denmark becomes a charter member of the United Nations.
1949	Denmark becomes a founding member of NATO.
1952	Denmark forms the Nordic Council with Finland, Iceland, Norway, and Sweden.
1973	Denmark joins the EEC along with Great Britain.
1992	The Maastricht Treaty is signed, creating the EU; Denmark initially rejects the treaty.
1993	A second Danish referendum ratifies the Maastricht Treaty.
2000	Denmark rejects a proposal to adopt the euro as its national currency.
2011	Social Democrat Helle Thorning-Schmidt becomes Denmark's first female prime minister.
2015	Lars Løkke Rasmussen returns as prime minister.
2016	Prime Minister Lars Løkke Rasmussen expands his minority government by forming a coalition with the Liberal Alliance and the Conservatives.

FURTHER READING & INTERNET RESOURCES

Further Reading

McCormick, John. *Understanding the European Union: A Concise Introduction.* London: Palgrave Macmillan, 2017.

Mason, David S. *A Concise History of Modern Europe: Liberty, Equality, Solidarity.* London: Rowman & Littlefield, 2015.

Russell, Helen. *The Year Living Danishly: Uncovering the Secrets of the World's Happiest Country.* London: Icon Books, 2016.

Steves, Rick. *Rick Steves Snapshot Copenhagen & the Best of Denmark.* Edmonds: Rick Steves' Europe, Inc., 2015.

Internet Resources

Denmark Travel Information and Travel Guide
www.lonelyplanet.com/denmark

Official Site of Denmark
http://denmark.dk

Denmark: Country Profile
http://www.bbc.co.uk/news/world-europe-17405422

Denmark: CIA World Factbook
https://www.cia.gov/library/publications/the-world-factbook/geos/da.html

The Official Website of the European Union
europa.eu/index_en.htm

Publisher's note:
The websites listed on this page were active at the time of publication. The publisher is not responsible for websites that have changed their addressees or discontinued operation since the date of publication. The publisher will review and update the website list upon each reprint.

INDEX

A
Aalborg, 22
Aarhus, 75–76
    Botanical Gardens, 77
    Old Town (Den Gamle By), 77
    Symphony Orchestra, 76
Afghanistan, 39
Agriculture, 14, 19, 21, 46–48, 49
Åland Islands, 36
Albani Brewery, 78
Almond butter balls, 63
Amalienborg Palace, 38, 73
Andersen, Hans Christian, 65, 66–67, 74, 78, 86
Anglican Church, 58
Animals, 18, 21
    marine life, 21
Apartments, 51
Area, 7
Aryans, 35
Austria, 33
Avedøre Power Plant, 50

B
Bak, Lars Ytting, 61
Baltic Sea, 10, 25, 84
Battle of Lyndanisse, 8
Bay of Køge, 15
Beaches, 13, 86
Beer, 45
    Carlsberg, 45
Belgium, 41
Bicycles, 82, 85. *See also* Cycling
Birth rate, 9
Blaavand, 13
Blixen, Karen, 65, 68, 69
Bluethooth, Harald, King, 27, 28, 29
Bohr, Niels, 65, 69

Bonaparte, Napoleon, 30–31
Borders, 7
Bornholm, 7, 10, 13
Bosnia and Herzegovina, 39
Bridges, 11
Brussels, 40
Buffet, 62
Burnet rose, 14

C
Canut, 28
Capital, 71
Carlsberg Brewery, 44, 74
Changing of the guards, 73
Charlemagne, 23, 24
Charlemagne (Dürer), 23
Children, 56
Christian
    I, King, 30
    IV, King, 30, 31
    of Oldenborg, Count, 30
Christiana, 88
Christianity, 27, 28
Christian IV of Denmark (Isaacsz), 31
Church of St. Nicholas, 71
Cities, 11, 71–78
Climate, 7, 16–17
Columbus, Christopher, 25
Commuters, 82
Concentration camps, 35
Concert Hall, 76
Constitution, 31, 36
Copenhagen, 8, 11, 25, 38, 44, 46, 48, 50, 52, 54, 59, 62, 70, 71–74, 82, 83, 86
    Jazz Festival, 73
Cormorant, 18
Cornfields, 11
Croatia, 39
Currency, 39, 49, 82

Cycling, 52, 61
Czechoslovakia, 33

D
Danes tribe, 24
Danish
    Baptist Church, 58
    language, 9, 24, 55
    meatballs, 63
    National Opera, 76
    Royal Life Guards, 38
Danneborg, 64
Danneborg, 8
Death rate, 9
Democracy, 31
Dinesen, Isak. *See* Blixen, Karen

E
Eastern Jutland, 16
Economy, 43–49, 83
    crisis, 39, 81
    expansion, 83
Education, 58, 60
Egypt, 39
Electricity, 49
Elevation, 7
Elsinore (Helsingør) Harbor, 42
"Emperor's New Clothes, The" (Andersen), 67
Energy, 48, 52–53, independence 81–82
    conservation, 52
    consumption, 52
    geothermal, 49
    passive house, 80
    progressive policies, 43
    wind, 53, 82, 84
Environment, protection of, 21
Eriksen, Eric, 74

INDEX

Esbjerg Port, 43
Estonia, 36
Ethiopia, 39
Ethnicity, 9
   homogeneous, 55
Euro, 39, 41, 82
European
   Coal and Steel
     Community, 41
   Community, 39
   Council, 40
   Economic Community, 41
European Union (EU), 11, 39, 46, 48, 82
   flag, 81
   formation, 40–41
   members, 41
   Parliament Building, 40
Exports, 49

F
Family structure, 56
Farming. *See* Agriculture
Faroe islands, 7, 8, 36
Faroese
   language, 9
   people, 9
Fertility rate, 9
FIFA World Cup, 60
Finland, 36
Fishing, 11, 42
Flag, 8, 64, 81
Flooding, 7
Food and drink, 62, 85. *See also* Beer
Football. *See* Soccer
Forest, 14, 18, 21
France, 24, 33, 40, 41, 61
Franks, 24
Frederik
   Crown Prince, 37
   I, 30
   II, 30
   IV, King, 31, 32
Frederik IV (Schiøtt), 32
Frikadellar, 63
Funen
   island, 65, 78
   Village, 78

G
Gallery of Decorative Arts, 77
Gas, natural, 48, 49, 52
Gastronomy, 85
Geography, 7
German language, 9, 24
Germans, 9
Germany, 7, 11, 24, 28, 33, 48, 86
Glaciers, 16
Godfred, 24
Gorm
   King, 27, 28
   the Old, King, 28
Great
   Britain, 33, 48. *See also* United Kingdom
   Depression, 33
Greenland, 7, 8, 36
Greenlandic language, 9
Gross domestic product (GDP), 44, 49
Guden river, 14, 16

H
Havneby, 11
Hazards, 7
Heating, 49, 50
Helle Thorning-Schmidt, 56
Hirtshals, 12
History, 23–41
   ancient, 23–24
Hitler, Adolph, 33
Holy Roman Empire, 30
Homes, 51
   eco-home, 80
   passive, 80
House of Oldenborg, 30
Hygge, 57

I
Ice age, 11–12
Iceland, 36
Immigration, 81
Imports, 49
Industries, 45–46, 49, 78
Information technology, 44
Inuit people, 9
Invasion, 31, 33
Iraq, 39
Iraqis, 9
Isaacsz, Pieter, 31
Isbjerget, 75
Islam, 9, 58
Island of Funen. *See* Funen, island
Islands, 8, 18, 21
Italy, 24, 33, 41

J
Jacobsen, Carl, 74
Jelling, 27
   Church, 27
   Stones, 26–27, 28
Jews, capture of, 35
Judaism, 35
Jutland, 13, 43
Jutland Peninsula, 8, 11, 12

K
Kenya, 68
Kierkegaard, Søren, 65, 69
Køge River, 15
   Path, 15

93

INDEX

Korea, 39
Kosovo, 39
Krone, 49, 82

L
Lakes, 16
Lammefjord, 7
Landscape, cultural, 14
Landsting, 36
Langelinie promenade, 74
Language, 9, 24, 55
    foreign, 58
Latvia, 36
Lego, 46
Legoland, 85
Lejre, 24
Liberal Party, 31
Life expectancy, 9
Lindholm Høje, 22
Literacy rate, 9, 58
Little Mermaid, 65, 74, 85
"Little Mermaid, The"
  (Andersen), 67
Location, 7
Lokken, 34
Loot Soudal Team, 61
Lutheran Evangelical
  Church, 58
Lutheranism, 28, 58
Lutherans, Evangelical, 9
Luxembourg, 41

M
Maastricht Treaty, 41
Madpakken, 62
Malmö, 54
Mandelsmørboller, 63
Map, 6
Margrethe II, Queen, 38
Marriage, 55
    paperless, 56
    same sex, 56

Marshland, draining or, 20, 21
Martial law, 35
Mary, Crown Princess, 37
Merger Treaty, 41
Methodist Church, 58
Migration rate, 9
Møn, 47
Monarchy, 8, 28, 29
    female right of
    succession, 36
    hereditary, 30
Moraine, 13
Mummification, 24
Munich Agreement, 33

N
Names, last, 56
Nationalism, 31
Nazi race ideology, 35
Netherlands, 41
Neutrality, 31, 33, 36
New Nordic Cuisine, 85
Nielsen, Carl, 78
"Nightingale, The"
  (Andersen), 67
Noma, 62
Nordic Council, 36, 39
North
    German Plain, 8
    Sea, 13, 25, 48
North Atlantic Treaty
Organization (NATO), 36
    operations, military and
    humanitarian, 39
Norway, 27, 36, 39, 48, 86
Nuclear bomb, 69
Nyhavn waterfront, 8, 72

O
Occupation, 34–35
Odense, 65, 67, 78, 79

Pilsner, 78
river, 14
Steel Shipyard, 78
Town Hall, 78
Oil, 48, 52, 81
    embargo, 81
Olympic medals, 60
Øresund Bridge, 54
Out of Africa (Blixen), 68

P
Paganism, 24
Parties, political, 31
Pentecostal Church, 58
People, 9, 55–69
    age, 9
Periodic table, 69
Pharmaceutical industry, 88, 89
Philosopher, 69
Plains, 12, 13
Plants, 18, 19, 21, 24
Poland, 10
Polish people, 9
Poppo the Monk, 29
Population, 11, 55
Population growth rate, 9
Prejudice, 81
Protestantism, 9

R
Recipe, 63
Redzepi, René, 62
Reformation, Protestant, 28
Religion, 9, 58
    freedom of, 58
Renaissance, 30
Resistance, 35
Rivers, 14
Rococo style, 73
Roman Catholicism, 9, 28, 58

INDEX

Romania, 60
Rømø, 11
Rosenborg Castle, 73
Roskilde
    Festival, 73
    Fjord, 17
Runes, 27
Russian Orthodox Church, 58

S
Salt, 13
Sandwiches, 62
Scandinavians, 9
Schiøtt, August, 32
Schleswig-Holstein, 36
Scientists, 69
Service industry, 44
Seventh Day Adventist Church, 58
Silkeborg, 16
    Langsø, 16
Skagerrak Strait, 12
Skjern river, 14
"Snow Queen, The" (Andersen), 67
Soccer, 60, 64
Social Democrats, 33
Socialism, 33
Social security system, 58
Somalia, 39
Soviet Union, 36
Sports, 58, 60
Standard of living, 58
Stor river, 14
Sudentenland, 33
Suffrage, 31
Sweden, 10, 11, 24, 36, 39, 48, 54, 82, 86
Swedish language, 24
Syrians, 9

T
Taxes, 82
    income, 58
Terrain, 7
Terrorism, 81
Thomsen, August Carl Vilhelm, 28
"Thumbelina" (Andersen), 67
Tivoli Gardens, 70, 85
Torvehallerne, 48
Tourism, 8, 10, 14, 15, 44, 65, 74, 85–88, 88–89. *See* Blixen, Karen
Transportation, 53
Treaties of Rome, 41
Treaty of Paris, 41
Trees, 18, 21
Turkish people, 9

U
"Ugly Duckling, The" (Andersen), 67
UNESCO World Heritage Site, 27
United Kingdom, 82. *See also* Great Britain
United Nations, 23, 36
    operations, military and humanitarian, 39
United States, 31
    relationship with, 88–89
University, 58

V
Valby, 44
Varde river, 14
Vendsyssel-Thy, 12
Viking
    house, 25
    meaning, 28
Viking Pageant, 73
Vikings, 22, 24, 75
    age of, 25, 28
Voting, 31

W
Waldemar II, King, 8
Weather. *See* Climate
Welfare state, 58
West Germany, 40, 41
Wind turbine, 43
World War
    I, 31
    II, 33–35, 40
Writers, 65–69

Y
Yding Skovhoej, 7

Z
Zealand, 11, 17

Picture Credits

All images in this book are in the public domain or have been supplied under license by © Shutterstock.com. The publisher credits the following images as follows:

Page 8, 38, 48: Kiev.Victor, pages 26-27 and 26 inset below: Carsten Medom Madsen, page 37: Marek Szandurski, page 40: Roman Yanushevsky, page 42: Nielskliim, page 44: Sergiy Papamarchuk, page 46: Lucian Milasan, page 52, 83: JJ Farq, page 55: J Lekavicius, page 57: Roman Babakin, page 51: EQRoy, page 52: Anton_Ivanov, page 63: DR Travel Photo and Video, page 75: Santi Rodriguez, page 79, 80: Roman Babin, page 598 Teodor Lazarev, page 60, 64: Salajean, page 61: Radu Razvan, page 62: Pe3K, pages 66-67 Mary 416, page 66 inset top: Paolo Bona: page 70: Mikhail Markoskiy; page 73: Pabkov, page 74: Andrey Shcherbukhin, page 75: Balipadma, page 76: Marc Lechanteur, page 80: Radovan1, page 85: William Perugini, page 87 LM Spencer.

To the best knowledge of the publisher, all images not specifically credited are in the public domain. If any image has been inadvertently uncredited, please notify the publisher, so that credit can be given in future printings.

Video Credits

Page 12 Geography Now!: http://x-qr.net/1D3q
page 24 TopTenz: http://x-qr.net/1G8Q
page 51 Journeyman Pictures: http://x-qr.net/1FTX
page 59 VisitDenmark: http://x-qr.net/1FtS
page 72 VisitDenmark: http://x-qr.net/1Guc

Author

Dominic J. Ainsley is a freelance writer on history, geography, and the arts and the author of many books on travel. His passion for traveling dates from when he visited Europe at the age of ten with his parents. Today, Dominic travels the world for work and pleasure, documenting his experiences and encounters as he goes. He lives in the south of England in the United Kingdom with his wife and two children.